To my son, Matthew, and the 2008-2009 Monday/Wednesday
WEE School class in Van Alstyne, Texas: Aerin, Alec, Blake, Bonnie,
Clay, Declan, Emory, Hannah, Isabella, Mackenzie, Parker, and Trey
for giving me this wonderful idea for a story.

Thank you Mom, Dad, and Eddy, for patience and love, Becky for all your expertise, and Ron for the wonderful book design and illustrations.

DAR

LCCN: 2009903939   Copyright ©2009 by Debbie Reece
ISBN 10: 06-1529072-8   ISBN 13: 978-0-615-29072-0

The Christmas Pumpkin

By Debbie Reece

Illustrated by Ron Head

Lia Cecile
A sweet story for you

Debbie Reece

It was a crisp fall day at Farmer Bill's pumpkin patch. The children were picking bright orange pumpkins to carve for Halloween.

There was one green pumpkin still on the vine.
Each pumpkin seemed to say, "Don't worry, you will
turn bright orange and get picked for Halloween."

But the pumpkin never turned bright
orange, and was not picked.

Fall turned to winter. When Farmer Bill went out to check his field, he found the green pumpkin all alone in the patch. He carefully plucked it from the vine and took it inside to his son, James.

"Ooh!" James squealed with excitement, "A Christmas Pumpkin! Thanks Daddy." James was beaming with the thought of a pumpkin for Christmas.

The next day at school James told his class about his special green pumpkin.

They all giggled. Even his teacher said, "A Christmas pumpkin? Who ever heard of such a thing?"

"We decorate bright orange pumpkins for Halloween.

We eat delicious pumpkin pies for Thanksgiving.

We decorate our yards with bright orange pumpkins in the fall.

But what would you possibly do with a pumpkin for Christmas?"

James went home and told his mother about his day. When she tucked him into bed she said, "Son, don't worry about what people say. I think it's a great idea. Tomorrow I will take you to the store and you can get some decorations for your Christmas Pumpkin."

That night James dreamed about his pumpkin.

Maybe I will string
colorful lights all
over it,

or wrap it in silver tinsel
and gold garland.

I could put a star on top
and hang ornaments on it!

The next day at the store, James told the clerk, "I want to decorate my pumpkin for Christmas."

The clerk replied with a giggle, "A Christmas pumpkin? Who ever heard of such a thing?"

"We decorate bright orange pumpkins for Halloween.

We eat delicious pumpkin pies for Thanksgiving.

We decorate our yards with bright orange pumpkins in the fall.

But what would you possibly do with a pumpkin for Christmas?"

James was sad because no one wanted to help him decorate his pumpkin.

As they turned to leave the store, a kind old man with a long white beard spoke to James. He pulled a stubby red candle from his pocket and said, "Why don't you take this with you." James didn't know what he would do with the little red candle, but thanked the old man anyway.

Then the man wished James and his mother a Merry Christmas... and winked.

That night, Farmer Bill called James into the kitchen. His mother had the pumpkin on the table. "James," she said, "I think your green pumpkin is a wonderful way to celebrate Christmas. We could cut a lid and scoop out the inside."

"And carve something on it like we do for Halloween," Farmer Bill said. They listened to Christmas carols playing on the radio while they carved and decorated the green pumpkin.

James had so much fun reaching in and pulling out all of the seeds. He wanted to carve a star on it. "So that it can shine like the star that the Three Wise Men followed to find baby Jesus in the manger!" he said with excitement.

When he finished, he placed the stubby red candle inside the pumpkin. James was so happy.

The pumpkin was perfect. He put it on the front porch for
everyone to see.

Each night people
would drive by and honk
when they saw the Christmas
Pumpkin. News spread fast and they
were on TV and even in the newspaper!

One night the local television station came to their house and did a special report on the "Christmas Pumpkin".

The news lady said with a giggle, "A Christmas Pumpkin! Who ever heard of such a thing?"

In the newspaper, there was a picture of James and his pumpkin.
The article read: We decorate bright orange pumpkins for
Halloween. We eat delicious pumpkin pies for Thanksgiving.
We decorate our yards with bright orange pumpkins in the fall.
But what would you possibly do with a pumpkin for Christmas?

On Christmas Eve, James tried to stay awake all night. He wanted to know what Santa thought of his pumpkin. He fell asleep, but the stubby red candle in his pumpkin burned all night, bright like a star.

The next morning when James woke up,

he found a letter from Santa.

Dear James,

A Christmas pumpkin? Who ever heard of such a thing? We decorate bright orange pumpkins for Halloween. We use bright orange pumpkins to decorate our yards in the fall and eat delicious pumpkin pies for Thanksgiving.

But you had faith in a green pumpkin and decorated it with a beautiful star to shine for all to see. Because of you, now everyone knows what a green pumpkin can do for Christmas.

Merry Christmas James.
Thank you for letting your light shine bright!

Love Santa

The next year, on a crisp fall day at Farmer Bill's pumpkin patch, the children were picking bright orange pumpkins to carve for Halloween.

They were also picking the green ones hoping they could have a Christmas Pumpkin...

Just like James.

Create your very own Christmas Pumpkin!

(Details on back)

Use this page to design your own Christmas Pumpkin.
You can send it to us and we will display it on our website at
www.beebopbooks.com.
Mail your Christmas Pumpkin to:

BeeBop Books
P.O. Box 1424
Howe, Texas 75495-1424